A B C's of CATS

Review the Alphabet While Learning About Cats

By Larry Hartford

Published 2023
KSO Publishing

Contact Larry Hartford at:
larryhartford@outlook .com

Dedicated to my Lord Jesus Christ, creator of the fascinating cat.

Also to my wife and children for their feedback and ideas for this book.

A is for Awesome

Cats make awesome pets and great friends.

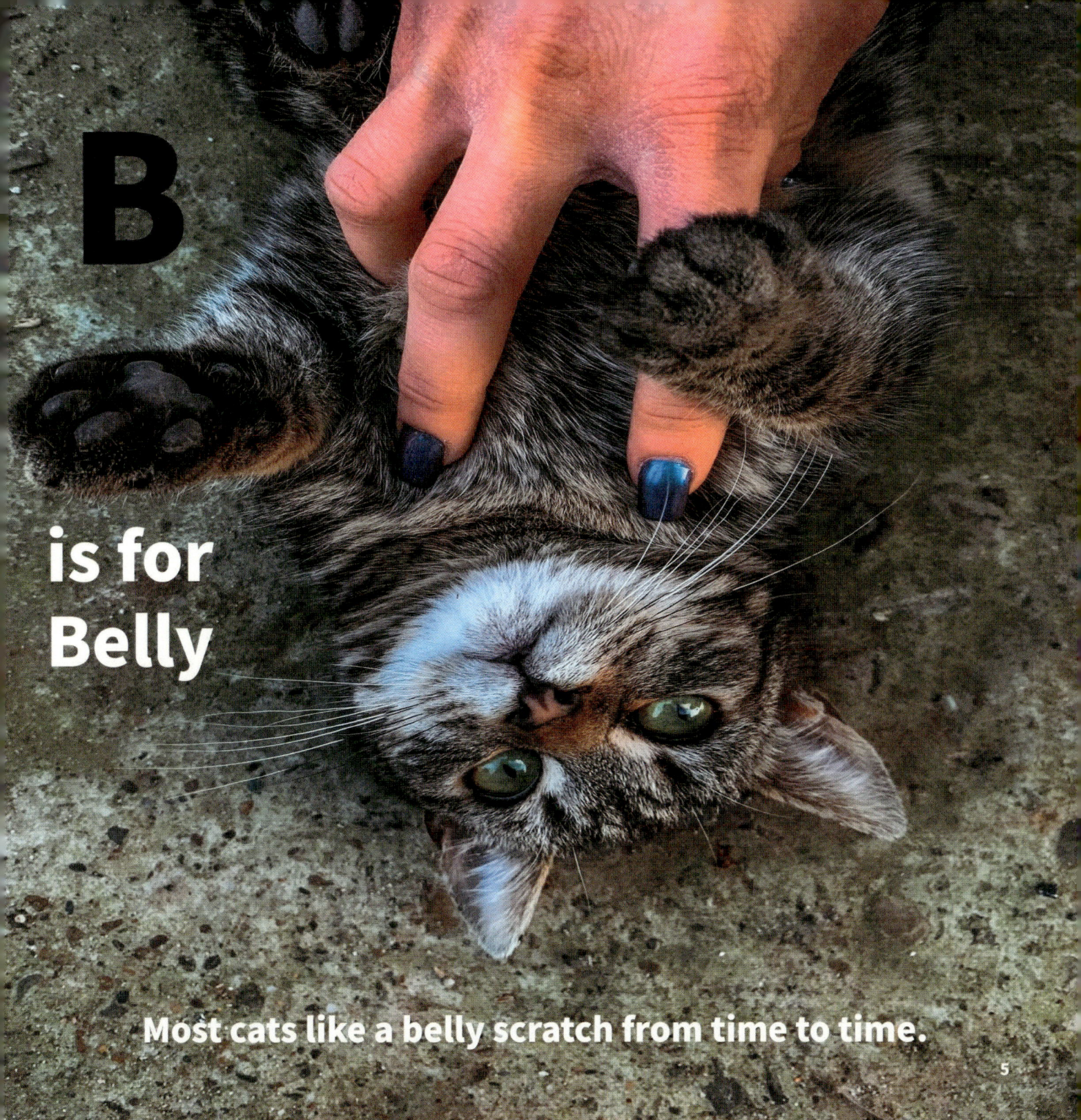

B
is for Belly

Most cats like a belly scratch from time to time.

C
is for Claws

Cats have sharp claws that they use for hunting, climbing, and defending themselves.

D is for Daring

Cats can be daring. Cats like to climb into high places such as trees and window ledges.

E is for Eyes

Cats have special eyes. They can see at night better than they can during the day. Wow!

F is for Fur

A cat's fur can be long or short. Fur helps a cat to keep warm in the winter, and cool in the summer.

G is for Growl

When cats sense danger, they growl as a warning to back off and go away.

H is for Huggable

Cats are huggable. They are so warm and soft, that people just want to hug and hold them. Not all cats like to be hugged though!

I is for Into

Cats like to crawl into things. They love to explore boxes, bags, cupboards, and other small spaces.

J
is for Jump

Cats can jump up onto high places. They can jump down and land on their feet.

K is for Kittens

When a mommy cat has babies, these babies are called kittens. Kittens are so small, soft, and cuddly!

L is for Lay

A cat will lay down when it wants to relax or sleep. Some cats curl up to form a ball shape. Others will lay straight across, and a few will even lay on their backs.

A cat meows in order to talk to you. A meowing cat might want to be fed, go outside, or have a belly scratch.

M
is for Meow

N is for Nose

A cat's tiny nose has a big sense of smell. Cats are always sniffing because they can smell odors that we could never smell.

O is for Outside

Some cats love to go outside. They like to explore and hunt. Cats rarely get lost.

P is for Paws

Cats have four paws that are great for catching mice. They can also use their paws for batting toys around the house, and to sneak up on you without making a sound!

Q
is for
Quick

Cats are very quick. They can run faster than people. Cats are so quick, they can snatch up a mouse in a blink of an eye!

R is for Ride

Some cats like to ride. Other cats hate riding.

S is for Silly

Cats can be very silly, chasing things like a string or a laser light. Sometimes, cats will chase each other and wrestle.

T is for Tail

A cat uses its tail for balance when jumping, running, or walking along narrow objects, like a fence.

U is for Urine

A cat's urine, or pee, has a very strong odor. Cats sometimes pee on things, to mark them as theirs. The strong odor warns other cats to stay away!

V is for Vet

A vet is a doctor for animals. Vets help to keep cats healthy.

W is for Whiskers

Whiskers help cats to not bump into things. Whiskers also help cats measure if they will fit into small spaces without getting stuck. That's pretty neat!

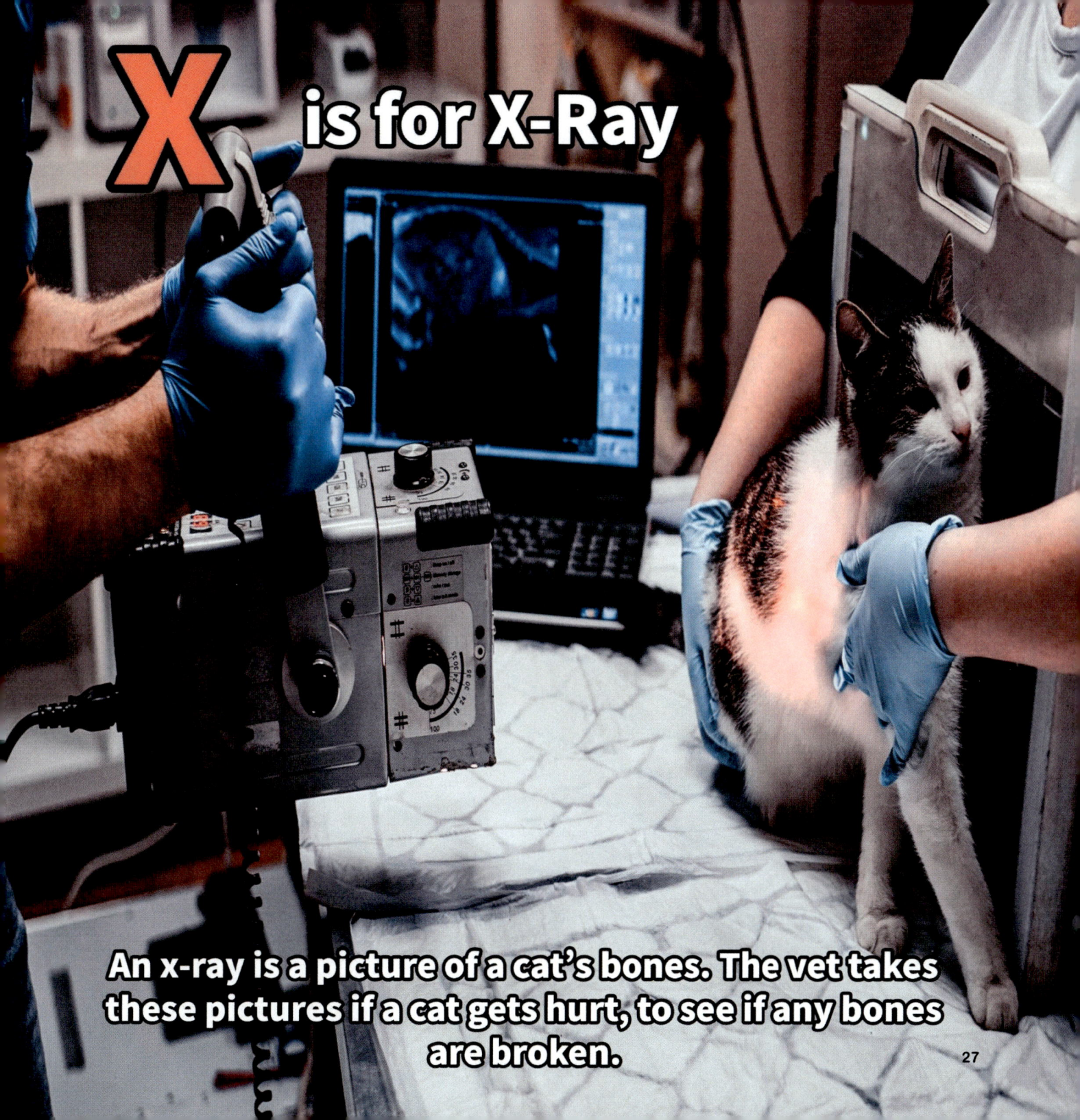

X is for X-Ray

An x-ray is a picture of a cat's bones. The vet takes these pictures if a cat gets hurt, to see if any bones are broken.

Y is for Yawn

Like you, cats yawn when they are relaxed, bored, or tired. A cat's yawn is a little shorter than a person's, and is usually followed by a sigh.

Z is for Zzz's

This means that the cat has fallen fast asleep and may be quietly snoring. This is sometimes referred to as, "catching some zzz's." Cats tend to sleep more during the day, but may also sleep in the middle of the night.

The End

A message from Larry Hartford.

Hello parent,

Thank you for purchasing this first book in the Look N Learn series. These books are designed to teach multiple concepts while your child enjoys the thought provoking pictures or illustrations.

If your child enjoyed this book, pleasee leave an honost review where you purchased it, or on Amazon.

Thank You!

Made in the USA
Coppell, TX
20 January 2026

69678282R00021